Career Exploration

Careers If You Like Social Interaction

Barbara Sheen

ReferencePoint Press®

San Diego, CA

© 2020 ReferencePoint Press, Inc.
Printed in the United States

For more information, contact:
ReferencePoint Press, Inc.
PO Box 27779
San Diego, CA 92198
www.ReferencePointPress.com

LIBRARY OF CONGRESS CATALOGING-IN-PUBLICATION DATA

Name: Sheen, Barbara, author.
Title: Careers If You Like Social Interaction/by Barbara Sheen.
Description: San Diego, CA: ReferencePoint Press, [2019] | Series: Career
   Exploration | Audience: Grade 9 to 12. | Includes bibliographical
   references and index.
Identifiers: LCCN 2018053852 (print) | LCCN 2018058020 (ebook) | ISBN
   9781682825945 (eBook) | ISBN 9781682825938 (hardback)
Subjects: LCSH: Professions—Vocational guidance—Juvenile literature. |
   Career development—Juvenile literature. | Social interaction—Juvenile literature.
Classification: LCC HD8038.A1 (ebook) | LCC HD8038.A1 S54 2019 (print) | DDC
   331.702—dc23
LC record available at https://lccn.loc.gov/2018053852

Contents

A Big Decision

Choosing a career is a big decision. Some young people seem to know exactly what they want to do with their lives from an early age. But many others feel stressed and clueless. Indeed, there is a lot of pressure on young people to settle on a career path while they are still in high school, even though many people do not figure out what they want to do until they are in their twenties or even older. And the fact that everyone seems to have an opinion about what path you should follow just makes things more confusing.

There is a good reason for the pressure. Without a clear sense of direction, individuals often waste years in a dead-end job that makes them miserable. Or they invest a great deal of time, effort, and money preparing for a career that is not right for them. It is not uncommon for unsatisfied workers to dread going to work each day. Once they are at work, they deal with boredom and frustration, and they lack the motivation and enthusiasm that helps people who enjoy what they do succeed in their career. As author Catherine Lovering explains, "Successful people are required to meet high performance standards. . . . From the most basic gauge of job happiness, from getting up in the morning to going to work because you love your job, to pushing yourself to go further in your career, remaining engaged is key to continued success."[1] Moreover, unhappiness and frustration with their work lives can spill over into people's personal lives and their sense of self-worth.

What Do You Like to Do?

Clearly, it makes sense for individuals to spend their work time doing something they enjoy. But how do you find a career that will make you happy? According to the Bureau of Labor Statistics, there are approximately twelve thousand different occupations to choose from. This prospect is exciting but also mind boggling. With so many options, there has to be a career that suits every individual's specific interests and skills. But learning about thousands of occupations in order to make an informed decision about what you want to do is an almost impossible task.

A good way to narrow down your choices is to identify the things you like to do, ask yourself why you like doing them, and then research careers that involve tasks you like. Say, for instance, your favorite activities include performing in a marching band, playing on a basketball team, and being a member of your student government. On the surface, these activities seem completely different. But by analyzing what you like about these activities, you'll find they share at least one common bond—they all involve working closely with other people. If this is an important reason why you enjoy these activities, you are probably a person who is best suited to a career with lots of social interaction, rather than one with little interpersonal contact.

People Skills Are in Demand

Not everyone has the skill or real liking for working with others. In fact, individuals who enjoy and are good at working with others are in demand in a wide range of industries and occupations. Some examples of jobs that entail lots of social interaction include mental health counselors, receptionists, life coaches, and real estate agents. College professors, lawyers, office managers, and speech therapists, among others, also fit into this category.

Many jobs that involve lots of social interaction also require candidates to have specific technical knowledge or skills, which individuals learn through education and training. For example, emergency medical technicians must be knowledgeable about medicine, but they also must be comfortable and good at dealing with a wide range of people. Indeed, if two candidates for a job have similar résumés, many employers prefer to hire the candidate who works well with others. As Vicki Salemi, a career expert for the job search website Monster and a former corporate recruiter, explains, "Companies want someone who's not only a stellar performer but who gets along with others, even difficult people."[2]

So if you thrive on social interaction, you can pursue a career doing what you like to do, knowing that recruiters are looking for people like you. Chances are, pursuing a career doing what you like will enhance both your personal and work life. As Mary Dowd, the director of student conduct at Minnesota State University, Mankato, explains: "Workers are most content when given an opportunity to use their skills and talents in a meaningful way."[3]

Event Planner

What Does an Event Planner Do?

If you've ever served on a prom committee or helped plan a *quinceañera* or other big party, you know that planning and putting on a special event is a major undertaking that takes lots of time and effort and involves dozens of different people. Event planners (also known as meetings, convention, and wedding planners) plan, coordinate, and manage every detail of corporate events such as conferences, conventions, trade shows, and employee appreciation programs. They also handle fund-raisers, political rallies, major sports and entertainment events, and personal events like weddings. By acting as a liaison between clients and the many vendors, suppliers, and other personnel needed to create and pull off a large social event, they take the stress off their clients so that their clients can relax and enjoy the results.

Starting with the initial planning and continuing until the last guest departs, these professionals coordinate and manage every aspect of a major event. Working with each client, they establish a realistic budget and carefully adhere to it. They research and book venues, caterers, florists, and entertainment. They negotiate and prepare contracts, plan menus, create event themes, coordinate decorations and favors, and supervise event personnel. From ensuring that every place setting is perfect to being on hand to monitor the actual event, event planners handle hundreds of large and small details in an effort to turn their client's vision into an unforgettable occasion. As Los Angeles wedding and event planner Lauren Spingola explains, "Seeing ideas on paper come to life, and the happiness on my clients' faces is the greatest feeling. I love creating happiness!"[4]

A Typical Workday

Event planners are busy people. Their workdays are jam-packed with a wide range of activities. Each day is different, depending on the type and number of projects they are tackling. So if you are an energetic person who gets bored with a set routine, this career may suit you to a tee.

Before starting work on any event, the first thing these professionals do is meet with the client to discuss the purpose of the event, the client's vision for the event, and the budget. Next, event planners contact possible venues and service providers and solicit bids from the most promising. Then, they prepare a proposal for the client. Once the date, time, and venue are settled on, event planners work on coordinating all the details. They negotiate contracts; sample foods and wines; choose flowers; and audition and hire entertainment, among other activities. "I don't know another job where you are allowed to try new foods, hear different bands and enjoy a variety of good cocktails and wines—all while working,"[5] says Seattle event planner Sheena Kalso.

Planning the event is only part of the job. On the day or evening of the event, these professionals can be found at the venue. Although they may blend in with the guests and look like they are there to have a good time (which they often do), they are present to make sure that everything goes off smoothly. Danielle Nunez Seaberg, president of Grand Events in Tampa, Florida, explains, "Even if there are no problems, someone needs to quarterback the event.

Caterers need to be shown to the kitchen, the DJ needs to know where to access electrical service, the valet people want to know if they can park on the grass, and it goes on and on."[6]

Education and Training

If you decide to be an event planner, you can start preparing for this career in high school by taking speech and language arts classes. Event planners need good written and oral communication skills in order to convey information to clients, vendors, and other business professionals. These classes help sharpen those skills. Classes in marketing and business are also useful. Many event planners are self-employed. Business and marketing classes help students learn how to prepare a business plan, run a business, and create marketing materials—skills that are vital to running a business. Computer science classes are also helpful. Event planners use social media, virtual meeting software, and spreadsheets in their work. They should therefore be comfortable using different computer applications.

After graduating from high school, there are a number of paths you can follow. This field is not regulated, and it is possible to enter it with a high school diploma; however, candidates with postsecondary education are more likely to get ahead in this

profession. Some individuals train for this profession by enrolling in an event-planning program offered online or by a vocational institute. These programs often take from four months to one year to complete. Others pursue an associate's degree with a major in hospitality management, which takes two years to complete. Others pursue a bachelor's degree with a major in hospitality management, business, or public relations. Although having a bachelor's degree is not required, many employers prefer to hire degreed candidates.

In addition to formal education, gaining experience in planning events gives candidates a leg up when it comes to getting hired. Serving on or chairing school, club, or other committees that plan dances, fund-raisers, and other special events is a good place to start. Working part time for a catering company or doing an internship with an event-planning agency are excellent ways to learn about event planning. And the experience looks great on your résumé.

Skills and Personality

Event planning is all about bringing people together. It is a very social profession. If you want to be an event planner, you should like working with others. Successful event planners need to be personable, tactful, and patient. Plus, they should have great communication and listening skills. Good listening skills help these professionals understand their clients' wants and needs, while good written and oral communication skills allow them to clearly convey this information to event personnel.

Being extremely organized, detail oriented, and a skilled multitasker are other vital qualities that event planners depend on. Event planners are like expert jugglers. At any given time, they have dozens of different balls (in the form of activities, deadlines, details, and multiple events) in the air. The pressure can be intense. These professionals must stay calm and focused no matter the circumstance. "Successful event planners need to know how to effectively multitask and keep many aspects of the event moving along simultaneously without any of those tasks falling by the wayside. . . . Being highly organized is a must for successful event planning,"[7] says Toronto event planner Melanie Woodward.

Creativity and problem-solving skills are also essential. Event planners create fun. It takes lots of creativity to come up with innovative and unique event themes and decorating ideas. As San Francisco event planner Tiffany Klein explains, "I like each party to have a twist, and I don't think I have done the same thing twice. . . . It's the little details—the jazz band that plays during cocktail hour, or vintage German beer coasters and beer steins at an Oktoberfest party—that make a party really special."[8] Plus, you must be able to think on your feet. Even the best-planned events do not always go the way they should. Should problems arise, event planners have to make rapid decisions concerning the best course of action to take.

Working Conditions

Most event planners work full time. Their work hours can be irregular. It is not unusual for event planners to work from early morning to late at night on the day of an event. They often work on weekends and holidays, too. And they are on their feet a lot.

This is a fast-paced profession for people who enjoy being on the go. Although event planners spend part of their time in an office, they also spend a lot of time at event venues and visiting vendors and suppliers. Not only do they travel locally, they may jet off to exotic locations to scout out prospective sites for destination weddings, conferences, and conventions. They often attend those events as well. Woodward explains, "I've planned events all over the world, hundreds and thousands of miles away from where I actually live. . . . The key is really to go down and source everything . . . meet the people, see the hotel, go to the restaurants, try the food . . . which can be a lot of fun too."[9]

Employers and Pay

Event planners are employed by event-planning agencies; business, religious, philanthropic, civic, educational, and professional organizations; resorts; and food service and recreational facilities. Many are self-employed. According to the Bureau of Labor Statistics (BLS), the median annual income for event planners in 2017 was $48,290. The lowest-paid 10 percent of these professionals earned less than $26,390 while the highest-paid 10 percent earned more than $82,980. Salaried event planners usually

A Really Big Event

"One of my favorite events was a festival that I helped plan, and there was over 30,000 people coming from across the country for this festival. And the reason I loved it so much was because there were 30,000 people coming from across the country and it had national attention, and there was media involved. And we had 750 volunteers that we had to interview and slot into positions that they were right for, that they had the skill level for."

Melanie Woodward, Toronto event-planning expert

Quoted in Tom Crowl, "Event Planning Tips with Melanie Woodward," *The Savvy Event Planner Podcast*, 2018. http://savvyeventpodcast.com.

receive employee benefits such as health insurance and paid sick leave and vacations. Self-employed event planners do not.

Future Job Outlook

The future looks bright for event planners. The BLS predicts that employment opportunities for event planners will increase by 11 percent through 2026, which is faster than the average growth rate for all professions. However, competition for the best positions can be fierce. Candidates with a bachelor's degree in a related field should have the best job opportunities. Being a certified special events professional and/or a certified meeting planner is also advantageous. Although certification is not required, these credentials, which are offered by various professional organizations, identify individuals as experts in the field, which can help them advance in their career. To gain certification, individuals must have event-planning experience and successfully complete an exam.

Find Out More

International Live Events Association (ILEA)
330 N. Wabash Ave., Suite 2000
Chicago, IL 60611
website: www.ileahub.com

The ILEA is a professional organization made up of business owners and current and aspiring event planners. It offers social, networking, and educational events; career information; and job postings and administers and awards credentials in event planning.

Meeting Professionals International (MPI)
2711 Lyndon B. Johnson Fwy., Suite 600
Dallas, TX 75234
website: www.mpiweb.org

The MPI is the world's largest professional organization for meeting and event professionals. It offers publications, a blog, industry updates, information about venues and vendors, and job postings. It administers and awards credentials in event planning.

QC Event School
7201 Wisconsin Ave., Suite 440
Bethesda, MD 20814
website: www.qceventplanning.com

QC is an online school for aspiring event planners. Besides offering classes, it provides lots of information about this career field on its website, including interviews with event planners, salary information, and articles about event planning.

Fitness Trainer and Instructor

What Does a Fitness Trainer and Instructor Do?

If you are passionate about fitness and want to make a positive impact on the health of others, a career as a fitness trainer and instructor may be right for you. Fitness trainers and instructors (also known as personal trainers and group exercise instructors) instruct, lead, coach, and motivate individuals in fitness activities that help participants improve their overall health and quality of life. As Vancouver personal trainer Ryan Murphy explains, "I love being a trainer because I can teach people how to use their training to create a healthier, happier version of themselves every day."[10]

These professionals work one-on-one with individuals, partners, or small groups as personal trainers, and they instruct group classes as exercise instructors. Some focus on one role, while others do both. In their role as personal trainers, upon meeting a new client, the first thing these fitness specialists do is review the client's medical history, assess the client's fitness level, and identify the client's fitness goals. Then they develop a customized training program designed to meet the client's unique needs. During each training session, personal trainers demonstrate proper exercise technique, monitor clients

Keeping Students Safe

"I teach a yoga-Pilates class in several different gyms. I have my own classes, and I also sub for other instructors. Before each class, I welcome everyone, describe the class if I have new participants, and might show them postures that they won't be able to see once class starts. During class, as I cue (explain) and demonstrate what we're doing, I also look around to see if anyone needs to make adjustments or corrections. I'll cue modifications or options as needed to make sure everyone is safe."

Tammy Kenney, group fitness instructor

Quoted in Kathleen Greene, "My Career," *Occupational Outlook Quarterly*, Winter 2012–2013. www.bls.gov.

as they exercise, and cheer their efforts. These professionals use exercise equipment such as free weights, resistance bands, exercise machines, and fitness balls as training tools. Through their efforts, personal trainers help people tone and strengthen their bodies, get in shape for a specific sport or activity, and improve physical functions impacted by injuries, aging, or health issues. They also advise clients about diet, nutrition, health, and weight control.

In their role as group fitness instructors, these experts plan, choreograph, and lead fitness classes designed to work various sets of muscles. Some group fitness instructors specialize in one or more particular form of exercise, such as spinning, yoga, or water aerobics, to name a few. By making classes fun, they try to motivate participants to adopt healthy exercise habits. Since group classes typically include people of varying fitness levels, during the class, instructors offer suggestions and adaptations to help make exercises suitable for all participants, no matter their capabilities or limitations. "I know that everyone gets something different out of my class," says Tammy Kenney, a Virginia exercise instructor. "Before they walk in, they're all coming in with different needs, so the class can't be one-size-fits-all. I have to tailor it to meet the needs of the people who are there."[11]

In addition to specializing in a particular form of exercise, some fitness professionals focus on working with specific populations. For instance, some fitness trainers and instructors work with athletes in an effort to improve their athletic performance. Others focus on older adults, instructing them in activities that improve balance and slow down muscle and bone loss associated with aging. Still others concentrate on helping people manage their weight through exercise and nutritional counseling.

A Typical Workday

If you enter this field, plan on being incredibly active. Fitness trainers and instructors are almost always on the move—demonstrating exercises, coaching clients, and leading classes. They may train five to ten people a day and teach multiple classes. Some days are busier than others. But even when these fitness experts are not training and instructing others, they are rarely idle. They have lots of administrative tasks to attend to. These include marketing their services, scheduling and billing clients, writing programs for clients, updating client data, and choreographing new exercise routines.

Education and Training

Education and training requirements for this career vary by employers and specialty areas. Almost all fitness trainers and instructors are high school graduates. Some have an associate's or bachelor's degree in kinesiology, exercise science, or physical education. If this career interests you, you can start preparing for it in high school by taking physical education classes, which help get and keep you in good shape. Classes in health and biology are also vital. They provide prospective fitness professionals with an understanding of the human body and its health and nutritional needs. A psychology class is another good choice. A big part of a fitness professional's job is to direct and motivate others. Knowledge of psychology helps trainers successfully do this.

In addition to high school classes, if you are interested in following this career path, you should be familiar with and skilled in different types of workouts and understand how various physical activities affect the body. Working out with a personal trainer and taking a variety of group exercise classes (and practicing consistently) are great ways to explore specialty areas, observe what fitness professionals do, learn proper exercise forms and techniques, and become more adept at fitness training and instruction. As Kenney explains, "You have to love it yourself before you can teach it to others. Go to a variety of classes. Find what you love. Be able to see yourself completely immersed in it."[12]

Although there is no national standard for entering this profession, many fitness facilities require that prospective trainers and instructors "audition" by teaching a group exercise class before being hired. In addition, many employers prefer that fitness instructors and trainers have national certification, which is offered by a number of fitness organizations. Requirements vary, depending on the certifying organization and the type of certification. Generally, to become certified as a fitness trainer and instructor, you must be at least eighteen years old and successfully complete a written exam that tests your knowledge of exercise science. In addition, fitness professionals are required to have cardiopulmonary resuscitation certification, which takes about three hours of training and is offered by the Red Cross and many community organizations.

Skills and Personality

If this is the career for you, you should be passionate about fitness and sharing the benefits of exercise with others, have knowledge of human anatomy, and be physically fit. The latter does not mean that you have to be ultra-ripped. But you do have to be strong and healthy. And since this is an occupation that involves almost constant social interaction, you should have excellent interpersonal skills and like working with people. Clients are drawn to trainers and instructors who are cheerful and likable. Personal trainers and fitness instructors rely on their interpersonal skills to connect with their clients, make them feel at ease, and motivate them. According to Anita Lemon, director of the Academy of Fitness Professionals, "The best trainers are natural inspirers of others. . . . They don't tell their clients what to do but instill a desire, confidence and determination that enables them to stick with their personal training course and achieve results."[13]

Working Conditions

Fitness trainers and instructors typically work indoors in fitness centers, exercise studios, and recreational facilities. They may also train clients and lead classes outdoors in parks and on beaches. Some fitness professionals work with clients in the clients' homes or workplace or work in more than one fitness facility, which involves traveling from place to place.

Fitness professionals work full and part time. In order to accommodate their clients' schedules, they often work irregular hours, as well as weekends and evenings. Since many people prefer to exercise before or after work, fitness professionals' day typically begins early in the morning and ends after dark. They usually have breaks throughout the day when they are not training clients or leading classes. During these times, they are usually free to come and go, depending on their employer. According to Lisa M. Wolfe, the author of six fitness books, "Working both morning and evening hours

It's Hard Work

"Even though I wear workout clothes to work every day, this is not an easy job. The hours can be absolutely grueling, namely due to the most demanded time slots in a typical workday schedule (early AM before work, late PM after work). Client cancellations and reschedules typically make for completely upended schedules week to week, making it difficult to have a normal schedule and social life. We don't scream at everyone. It's not a television show. . . . It's not glamorous, it's just consistent hard work."

Christopher Huffman, certified personal trainer and strength and conditioning specialist; owner of Volition Fit, Garden City, Idaho

Quoted in Andy Orin, "Career Spotlight: What I Do as a Personal Trainer," Lifehacker, September 8, 2015. https://lifehacker.com.

may mean that you don't work five days a week. Or, you may work some mornings and some evenings but not both on the same day. You may work shorter hours six days a week to expand your morning and evening availability. Typically, trainers have the flexibility to manage their own schedules."[14]

Employers and Pay

According to the Bureau of Labor Statistics (BLS), 59 percent of fitness trainers and instructors are employed by fitness, recreation, and sports centers, and 11 percent are self-employed. Other employers include civic and social organizations, public and private educational services, and the government. The BLS reports that in 2017, the median annual income for this profession was $39,210. The lowest-paid 10 percent of these professionals earned less than $19,640, while the highest-paid 10 percent earned more than $74,520. Many fitness trainers and instructors begin their career as salaried employees. Once they gain experience and a client base, they may open their own fitness studios, which can be quite lucrative.

What Is the Future Outlook for Fitness Trainers and Instructors?

If you love fitness and sharing the benefits of exercise with others, you should be welcomed into this profession. Employment opportunities for fitness trainers and instructors are expected to grow by 10 percent through 2026, which is faster than average. This is because more people are becoming aware of the health benefits of exercise. According to the BLS, employment opportunities should be best for certified individuals, yoga and Pilates instructors, and those with postsecondary training.

Find Out More
American Council on Exercise (ACE)
4851 Paramount Dr.
San Diego, CA 92123
website: www.acefitness.org

ACE is a nonprofit organization that promotes good health through physical activity. It certifies group fitness instructors and personnel trainers, offers certification test study guides, and provides online education opportunities. It also provides interviews with fitness professionals and information about fitness, exercise, and health.

National Federation of Professional Trainers (NFPT)
530 Main St.
Lafayette, IN 47901
website: www.nfpt.com

The NFPT is an organization that certifies personal trainers. It offers test preparation materials and information about what personal trainers do, how to become a personal trainer, salaries, and work settings, as well as a variety of publications, articles, and a blog.

National Strength and Conditioning Association (NSCA)
1885 Bob Johnson Dr.
Colorado Springs, CO 80906
website: www.nsca.com

The NSCA is a professional organization of personal trainers, strength coaches, and others interested in strength and fitness. It certifies personal trainers, provides study guides and educational material, and offers a variety of articles, videos, and publications on fitness, personal training, and nutrition.

PersonalTrainerEDU.org
website: www.personaltraineredu.org

PersonalTrainerEDU.org is a website that supports current and aspiring fitness professionals. It offers career, certification, and salary information, among other resources. It also provides information about different fitness instructor specialty areas.

Hairstylist and Barber

What Does a Hairstylist or Barber Do?

Are you creative and artistic? Do you like working with hair, interacting with people, and helping others look and feel their best? If so, you might consider pursuing a career as a hairstylist or barber. Barbers' services are geared toward men, while hairstylists work on males and females.

From simple trims and buzz cuts to elaborate updos and fades, barbers and hairstylists (also known as hairdressers, cosmetologists, or beauticians) cut and style hair in order to improve people's appearance. Hairstylists also provide other beauty services, including applying chemical treatments that change the hair's color or texture, while barbers also shape and trim facial hair and offer hot lather shaves. Both advise clients about hair care and hair care products. Through their work, they enhance their clients' appearance and boost their self-confidence. According to hairstylist and blogger Barb Quinn, being a hairstylist "is more than just about hair. . . . It's about helping the ladies and gents who sit in your chair find their beauty, inside and out."[15]

Some hairstylists and barbers are generalists, while others concentrate on specialty areas. For example, some hairstylists limit their services to cuts and styles. Others specialize in hair coloring. Some focus on children or on hair services like braiding and making dreadlocks. Some barbers concentrate on hair art. They cut and shave intricate patterns and team logos, among other designs, into hair.

The Workday

When you are a barber or hairstylist, there are no "typical" days, but there are certain activities that most hair care professionals do on a daily basis. When they arrive at work, one of the first things they do is check their appointment book so that they know how many clients they are seeing that day. When their first client arrives, they consult with the client about what he or she wants done. If the individual is a new client, they ask questions about the client's lifestyle and the amount of time and effort the client plans to put into maintaining his or her hairstyle. As Encinitas, California, hairstylist Jenn Tandarich explains, "The more questions that are asked the better to ensure both the client and stylist are on the same page."[16] Barbers and hairstylists may also give recommendations about whether a specific cut, color, or chemical procedure would work for the client based on the client's lifestyle and hair texture.

Then they get to work on the client's hair. Unless the client prefers to relax and zone out while these beauty specialists are working, they usually chat with clients, which helps put customers at ease. It is not unusual for barbers and hairstylists to retain the same clients for years. As a result, they often come to know a lot about their clients' lives and families. As New York hairstylist Shane Michael explains, "People do wind up telling you a lot. They tell you about their relationships, about their family histories, about their health."[17]

Depending on their employer and the type of services they offer, hairstylists and barbers may work on as many as ten clients per day. They may see customers strictly by appointment or provide services to people who walk in without an appointment. Between clients, they sweep up hair and clean their workstation and their tools. To stop the spread of germs, they disinfect their equipment and wash their hands between each client. They also maintain records of their clients' contact information and the services they provide each client, which serves as a guide during future visits.

Education and Training

If you decide to become a hairstylist or barber, you should be a high school graduate and have successfully completed an accredited barber or cosmetology program (also known as beauty school). These programs are offered in postsecondary vocational institutes and take nine to fifteen months to complete. In preparation, it is helpful to take chemistry, art, and speech classes in high school. Hair care professionals work with a variety of chemicals. To prevent damaging clients' hair, they should understand how the chemicals they use work and how they react to different types of hair, which is where knowledge of chemistry kicks in. Art classes, too, are vital. Hairstylists and barbers are artists whose medium is hair. Art classes help them learn about color, balance, and design, all of which are essential to their work. And since hairstylists and barbers spend a lot of time talking with their clients, they should have good verbal communication skills. A speech class helps hone these skills.

Postsecondary course work includes classes in business practices, hair science, hair care practices, and infection control. Students learn technical skills and get hands-on experience in cutting and styling hair, as well as safety and sanitation procedures. Cosmetology students also practice applying color and chemical treatments, while aspiring barbers practice shaving, trimming, and shaping facial hair. At first, students practice on mannequins. As they become more adept, they work on clients in school-run hair salons and barbershops. The training is not easy. Students must complete an average of fifteen hundred training hours to graduate. In an interview on Momentum, a career advice website, Joanna, an experienced hairstylist, explains, "People assume that hairdressers are unintelligent and that it is a job that is easy to do and is a sort of 'fallback' job that people do when they can't do anything else. The training is actually very intensive and needs intelligence and skill to become a good and competent hairdresser."[18]

Upon graduating, students take either a barber or hairstylist licensing exam that includes a written and practical test. In some states, graduates of either program can take both exams and obtain both licenses.

Skills and Personality

Barbers and hairstylists are creative, artistic people. To succeed in this career field, you need to have an understanding of and an eye for color and design. You also need steady hands and good eye-hand coordination to "paint" on color and trim away teeny hairs. And you should be creative enough to visualize a hairstyle for even the worst tangle of hair.

Since this is an occupation that involves almost constant social interaction, good interpersonal skills are essential, too. Clients are drawn to stylists and barbers who are warm and friendly. In fact, hair care professionals depend on their people skills to help build and retain their client base. "People pay good money for your services and you don't have the right to be sad or stressed,"[19] advises El Paso, Texas, hairstylist Juliana Jimenez. Hair professionals also rely on their listening skills. They must listen carefully to what their client wants done in order to ensure that the client's wishes are fulfilled.

Being physically fit is another characteristic you need in this occupation. Hairstylists and barbers are on their feet a lot. You

A big part of the job of any hairstylist or barber is talking with clients—and not just about hair. Hairstylists and barbers spend a lot of time talking with clients about family, jobs, and vacations, among other topics.

need a lot of stamina to do this job. And you should look neat and well groomed. As hairstylist Salomé de Wet explains, "No one wants to go to a stylist that doesn't look the part themselves."[20]

Working Conditions

Hairstylists and barbers work indoors in well-lit barbershops and hair salons. They may work with many other professionals or in one-person facilities. Most work full time, but opportunities for part-time work also exist. In order to accommodate their clients' schedules, they usually work some evenings and Saturdays or Sundays. Those who are self-employed set their own hours.

These professionals twist and bend a lot and perform repetitive motions with their hands. This puts them at risk for musculoskeletal injuries and disorders, particularly of the wrist, thumb, and spine. In addition, they are exposed to a variety of chemicals that can cause skin irritation. To protect themselves, they wear smocks and disposable gloves.

Employers and Pay

Most barbers and hairstylists begin their careers as salaried employees in barbershops, hair salons, and large haircutting franchises. After working for several years and developing a loyal client base, 43 percent become self-employed. Self-employed hair professionals may open their own salon or shop, rent chair space in an existing hair salon or barbershop as an independent contractor, or become mobile hairdressers who visit clients in their homes. Unlike salaried employees, self-employed individuals are responsible for purchasing their own hair care products and supplies, doing their own scheduling, keeping financial records, and marketing their business. They may also manage other beauty professionals.

According to the Bureau of Labor Statistics (BLS), in 2017 the mean annual salary for barbers and hairstylists was $24,850, with the lowest-paid 10 percent earning less than $18,170 and the highest-paid 10 percent earning more than $50,670. These figures do not include tips, which can be quite generous. Salaried employees usually receive employee benefits like health insurance and paid sick leave and vacations. Self-employed individuals do not.

A Social Profession

"A lot of our work is also dependent on our personality. I have to be able to talk easily with people. It's like being on a first date all the time. Sometimes I have to just grin and bear it with people who I don't like. But it's social, which I really like."

Lynnae Duley, Chicago hairstylist

Quoted in Matthew Blake, "Hairstylist: 'It's Like Being on a First Date All the Time,'" *In These Times*, June 9, 2014. http://inthesetimes.com.

Future Job Outlook

The BLS reports that employment for barbers and hairstylists will grow by 13 percent through 2026. This is faster than average. Indeed, as long as people want to look and feel their best, this career field should thrive. Therefore, if working with hair is your passion, your future looks bright.

Find Out More

Beauty Schools
website: https://beautyschools.com

This website provides a comprehensive guide to barber and cosmetology schools and information about the programs each school offers. It also gives information about a variety of beauty industry careers, including barber and hairstylist, and information related to licensing, pay, and future outlook.

Cosmetologist Life
website: www.cosmetologistlife.com

This website provides a lot of information about what it is like to be a hairstylist, including information about landing a job, building clientele, cosmetology schools, and licensing.

Hairfinder
website: www.hairfinder.com

This website offers a wide range of information about hair and hairstyling, including many articles about becoming a hairstylist, cosmetology schools, and a career as a hairstylist.

Professional Beauty Association (PBA)
15825 N. Seventy-First St., Suite 100
Scottsdale, AZ 85254
website: https://probeauty.org

The PBA is a nonprofit organization representing cosmetologists and cosmetology students. It offers scholarship opportunities, industry news, licensing information, and various publications.

Human Resources Specialist

A Few Facts

Number of Jobs
About 547,800 as
of 2016

Pay
About $35,810 to
$103,570

**Educational
Requirements**
Bachelor's degree

Personal Qualities
Detail oriented, good
decision-making
skills

Work Settings
Indoors in an office
setting

Future Job Outlook
Projected 7 percent
job growth through
2026

What Does a Human Resources Specialist Do?

If you have ever had a job interview, it is likely that the person who interviewed you was a human resources specialist (also known as an HR specialist or HR professional). Serving as a link between employers and employees, HR specialists oversee personnel and labor relations for businesses and other organizations. By keeping workers safe, motivated, and happy, they help organizations succeed. As Heather Clark, director of human resources at the Huntzinger Management Group, explains, "When I can satisfy my superiors and my employees, it is a job well done. Nothing is more gratifying."[21]

These men and women perform many tasks. One of the most important is hiring personnel. Working with managers and top executives, HR specialists identify an organization's staffing needs, then they recruit, interview, and hire workers. As part of this process, they review résumés, perform background checks, and assess candidates' skills.

Once candidates are hired, HR professionals conduct orientation sessions to familiarize new employees with company policies. They also provide ongoing training and development for other employees. And they help new and existing employees set up and maintain insurance and pension plans. In many organizations, HR specialists oversee payroll, too.

Creating and organizing wellness programs and workplace perks such as free snacks, chair massages, and staff softball teams, which help attract and retain workers, also fall under HR. These professionals also make sure that the organization complies with all local, state, and federal regulations, which helps ensure workplace safety and fairness. Plus, they handle all employee relations issues. When workers have a problem such as harassment allegations, unfair treatment, or other issues, they report the problem to an HR specialist whose job it is to analyze the problem and come up with a fair solution.

HR professionals have other responsibilities, too. Using special software, they maintain employees' records concerning hiring, termination, transfers, and promotions. In fact, they often conduct employees' performance reviews. And they are typically involved in terminating ineffective workers and coordinating the exit process when people leave the organization for any reason. In addition, they are responsible for helping develop and implement the organization's strategic plans and goals. Indeed, these men and women have such a wide range of responsibilities that Ryan, an HR professional, jokingly describes himself as "a one man army."[22]

HR specialists can be generalists, like Ryan, who handle all aspects of human resources, or they can concentrate on a particular aspect of the field. Those who specialize may focus on staffing and recruitment, training and development, workplace safety, compensation and benefits, HR information systems, or employee relations.

The Workday

If you decide to be an HR specialist, you probably won't be bored. Each workday consists of a broad mix of activities, and each day is different. HR specialists' specific duties depend on the type and size of the organization they work for and whether they are generalists or specialists. As Sharlyn Lauby, an HR professional

Every Day Brings Something New

"So you ask . . . what is a typical day on the job? Hundreds of emails and other virtual communications, that can't wait, and guarantee that you will be faced with the balance between what needs to be done and what needs to be done faster! but, There is no typical day! Every day is different and every day means a new challenge in my world. Whatever 'checklist' I thought I was going to accomplish, rest assured will need to be changed by the end of each work day."

Heather Clark, director of human resources at the Huntzinger Management Group

Quoted in Melissa Suzuno, "Thinking of Working In HR? What You Need to Know," *After College* (blog), June 11, 2014. http://blog.aftercollege.com.

and blogger, explains, "If I were to ask twenty HR pros how they spend their time, I'd get twenty different answers."[23]

No matter what specific duties HR professionals are assigned, much of their workday is spent interacting with people. They attend several prescheduled meetings almost every day, in which they meet with supervisors, department heads, and high-level executives to discuss a variety of topics. These include but are not limited to staffing needs, compensation and payroll issues, safety measures, and employee performance. "A quarter of my day is spent in meetings,"[24] says Juanita, an HR manager. Other meetings are unscheduled but are equally important. These are typically with disgruntled employees who have a work-related problem to report.

Performing administrative tasks such as preparing reports and performance evaluations and maintaining and updating employee records also fills up the workday, as do recruitment and staffing matters. On any given day, these professionals may be found attending job fairs, creating and placing job postings online, combing through résumés, and conducting interviews. As Carly, an HR specialist with a financial services company, explains: "I spend a lot of my morning sorting through resumes. . . . Much of my afternoon is spent on initial phone interviews with qualified candidates. I schedule blocks of time each day for these meetings, pack them in back to back and cross my fingers that everything sticks to schedule."[25]

Education and Training

To land a job as an HR specialist, you need a bachelor's degree in human resources, business, management, psychology, or a related field. You can start preparing for this career in high school by taking a psychology class, which can help you understand and motivate coworkers. Speech and language arts classes are useful, too. HR specialists rely on their oral and written skills to prepare reports, give presentations, conduct interviews, and explain difficult things clearly and concisely. Being adept at using computers, social media, databases, and specialized HR software is also vital. Computer science classes help boost these skills. And since these professionals work with numbers when dealing with budget matters and employee benefits, classes in business math are also helpful.

In college your coursework should include classes in human resources, business management, economics, finance, psychology, personnel administration, labor relations, employment law, and business writing. An understanding of these subjects helps prepare candidates to deal with the many components of this occupation.

Skills and Personality

HR professionals are versatile individuals. It takes a wide range of skills and personal qualities to succeed in this field. Open-minded, tactful people with excellent interpersonal skills have an advantage. If you pursue this profession, you can expect to work with people of diverse backgrounds. HR specialists must be able to get along well with others, no matter their gender, ethnicity, religion, age, or ranking in the company. Open-mindedness also comes into play in conflict resolution. In handling disputes, HR pros must be able to view things from both parties' perspective.

Integrity and confidentiality are other essential character traits. HR specialists are privy to confidential information, like their co-

A human resources specialist talks with a new hire about company policies and benefits. Human resources specialists may be involved in hiring, firing, and helping to sort out workplace problems.

workers' Social Security numbers, salaries, and performance ratings. In addition, it is not uncommon for individuals to share personal problems that impact their work life with HR personnel. Disclosing confidential information is an ethical violation, which can cause difficulties between coworkers and within an organization. It can also undermine rapport and trust between the HR department and other employees.

Being detail oriented is also essential. HR specialists must pay careful attention to detail when they perform background checks, evaluate job candidates' qualifications, maintain employee records, and make sure that the workplace is in compliance with governmental regulations. Even small oversights can lead to big problems. They must also be active listeners who pay careful attention to details while interviewing job candidates and handling conflicts. Plus, they must have good decision-making skills in order to hire the best candidates and solve big and small personnel and organizational problems.

Making Things Better

"The spirit of HR pros is always about improvement and how to make things better—whether we're talking about development, recruiting talent, developing benefit plans, looking at new HR tech tools or making HR processes more efficient, it's an area where we are always looking at raising the bar and taking people or processes to the next level."

Andrea Devers, HR technologist and change management expert

Andrea Devers, "10 Reasons Why I Love Being an HR Professional," Workology, February 10, 2015. https://workology.com.

Working Conditions

HR professionals work in an office environment. Some, especially those who specialize in staffing and recruiting, travel extensively to job fairs on college campuses. Most work a traditional five-day, forty-hour workweek. In large organizations, these men and women are usually part of a multiperson HR department and often work as part of a team.

Employers and Pay

HR specialists are employed by virtually every industry imaginable, ranging from businesses that manufacture and sell goods, to public and private organizations that provide a myriad of services, including health care, education, the military, and the government, to name a few. Some HR professionals are employed by personnel consulting firms that handle HR services for businesses and organizations that do not have an internal HR department. These include but are not limited to employment agencies, executive placement services, and temporary help services. Since HR professionals are used in almost every field, if you decide to become an HR specialist and you have a particular area of interest, you can combine your passions. So, for example, if you're crazy about cars, you can pursue an HR career in the automobile industry.

Wages for this profession vary based on the type of industry, employer, location, and the individual's education, experience, and areas of expertise. According to the Bureau of Labor Statistics (BLS), the median annual salary for HR specialists was $60,350 in 2017, with the lowest-paid 10 percent earning less than $35,810 and the highest-paid 10 percent earning more than $103,570. In addition, most HR professionals receive employee benefits, such as health insurance and paid sick and vacation days.

What Is the Future Outlook for HR Specialists?

The BLS reports that employment for HR specialists is expected to grow by 7 percent through 2026. This is about as fast as average for all occupations. Although competition for HR jobs is strong, if this sounds like a career for you, bucking the competition may be well worth the trouble. A recent survey of HR professionals conducted by the Society for Human Resource Management found that 86 percent of those surveyed reported high job satisfaction. As Leanne, an HR specialist, says, "I honestly love it, and can't see myself doing anything else!"[26]

Find Out More

After College
website: http://blog.aftercollege.com

After College is a blog dedicated to helping people explore career options and find a job. It has information about lots of different career fields, including human resources.

HumanResourcesEDU.org
website: www.humanresourcesedu.org

HumanResourcesEDU.org is an organization that serves as a resource for current and prospective HR specialists. It provides information about HR degree programs, state-by-state employment information, and salaries, as well as a scholarship database and career profiles.

Society for Human Resource Management
website: www.shrm.org

The Society for Human Resource Management is a professional organization made up of HR professionals from 162 countries. It offers information about this career, scholarships, career preparation, job postings, publications, webcasts, and voluntary certification for HR specialists.

Workology
website: https://workology.com

Workology is a website that provides information, articles, and podcasts for aspiring and current HR professionals, tips for HR job seekers, and general information about this career.

K-12 Teacher

What Does a K-12 Teacher Do?

Do you love learning and helping others learn? Does interacting with people, especially children or teens, make you happy? If so, you might consider a career as an elementary or secondary (K-12) teacher. K-12 teachers have many responsibilities, but their primary task is instructing students in academic subjects. They also help students develop social, study, organizational, and critical-thinking skills.

Teachers have the option of instructing a specific age group and/or subject. So if working with young children puts a smile on your face, you might want to teach elementary students. Or if you are passionate about a particular subject, you can focus on teaching it to secondary students. Most elementary teachers teach a mix of core academic subjects (language arts, math, science, and social studies) to the same group of students throughout the school day. Some teach only one academic subject to children in a particular grade level, such as fifth-grade language arts. Others specialize in teaching a noncore subject, such as physical education, art, or music to multiple grade levels. Secondary teachers usually concentrate on teaching a specific

A Middle School Spanish Teacher's Day

"The majority of my day is spent teaching both sixth grade and eighth grade Spanish. Depending on the day, I also have lunch duty or a department meeting for us to discuss curriculum, common assessments, or other department-related information. There is a small portion of my day that is spent communicating with parents and/or students. Students ask a lot of questions on Edmodo [an education website that connects teachers and students] and parents e-mail their questions or concerns. At the end of some school days, I help with afterschool activities."

Lisa Butler, Pennsylvania middle school Spanish teacher

Quoted in Teacher Certification Degrees, "Interview with Lisa Butler, Middle School Spanish Teacher and Faculty Member at Harrisburg University," 2018. www.teacher certificationdegrees.com.

subject to one or more grade levels. As a middle school music teacher explains, "Basically I teach sixth through eighth grade band. And I also teach eighth grade general music."[27]

In most states, teachers are licensed to teach either elementary or secondary school. Generally, elementary teachers are licensed to work with children in kindergarten through grade eight, and secondary teachers are licensed to instruct students in grades seven through twelve. This allows both elementary and secondary school teachers to instruct middle school students. But no matter the grade or subject area, to be successful, teachers must be able to connect with students and make learning interesting.

One way teachers do this is by creating and presenting lessons that students can relate to. This takes careful planning. Preparing and presenting lessons is just one of the many tasks that teachers perform. They also read and grade students' work, tidy and decorate the classroom, confer with parents and other educators, attend meetings, and complete loads of paperwork. Plus, they give students emotional support. As Texas elementary teacher Emily E. Smith explains, "On many occasions I play both educator and caretaker, which I admit can make one feel stretched thin at times, but I can't imagine shutting the door to my classroom and leaving all the troubles of my kiddos behind."[28]

A Typical Workday

If you decide to become an elementary or secondary teacher, you can expect lots of surprises. "Every day," according to third-grade teacher Dana Richliew, "brings something new. Whether it's a new challenge, a new concept to teach, or an off-the-wall comment by a silly kid, each day is completely different than the one before."[29]

Yet there are certain tasks that are a part of most teachers' workdays. For example, even before the first bell rings, teachers are busy getting ready for the day ahead. They make copies of work sheets, post assignments, gather supplies, and tidy up the classroom. As high school biology teacher Chad DeVoe explains, "The school day starts at 8:05 but I usually come in an hour early to set labs up or clean from the previous day."[30]

Once the school day begins, teachers in the lower grades can be found greeting students at the classroom door. Next they deal with administrative tasks like taking attendance and collecting parent-teacher correspondence. After teachers give a lesson, students get to practice new skills. While kids are working, teachers move around the classroom, helping individual students.

Teachers' schedules differ depending on the grade level they teach. High school and middle school teachers usually teach five or six forty-minute classes each day or two or three eighty-minute classes. Elementary teachers typically allot a designated amount of time for each subject, then move on to the next. Tennessee first-grade teacher Dana Lester explains, "We start our day with 90 minutes of reading. . . . [Then] we have handwriting, grammar, and then lunch. After lunch, I teach 90 minutes of math. . . . Then comes science or social studies . . . recess, and dismissal."[31]

K–12 teachers usually have one planning period and a thirty-minute duty-free lunch each day. During planning periods, they grade papers, plan lessons, communicate with parents, and collaborate with other educators, among other activities. When they are not teaching or planning, they may be assigned noninstructional duties such as monitoring students' behavior in the cafeteria.

Education and Training

K–12 teachers are required to have a minimum of a bachelor's degree from an accredited teacher education program. So if you decide to become a teacher, you can start preparing for the future by taking college preparatory classes in high school. Doing a high school service learning project in which you tutor children or adolescents is also a great idea. It is a good way to test whether you like teaching others.

College course work depends on the state, the university, and your field of interest. Generally, students major in education with a minor in a specific subject or vice versa. Students get practical hands-on experience by doing a semester of student teaching under the supervision of an experienced teacher. In addition, after earning a bachelor's degree, they must pass a background check and a licensing exam in order to be employed by public (and most private and parochial) schools.

Personal Qualities

If you want to become a teacher, plan on being a leader and a role model. Some kids spend almost as much quality time with their teachers as they do with their parents. What you say (both verbally and through body language) and your behavior, attitude, and appearance all have an impact on your students. To ensure that the impact is positive, teachers must practice self-control. Even when students act out, teachers must remember that they are the adult and present a calm, cool exterior. They should also dress professionally and be empathetic and respectful of every student no matter the student's behavioral issues or cultural differences. As Nevada first-grade teacher Alicia Lochridge explains, "Never doubt

Students listen to their teacher's explanation of a science experiment. K–12 teachers have to be able to make complex topics understandable and interesting for students who have different abilities and interests.

the impact you have on a child's life. You might be the only positive thing they experience that day. You will forever leave an imprint on each little soul. That is a huge and wonderful responsibility."[32]

Patience and creativity are essential, too. Students function on different levels, and not every learner understands new concepts right away. This can be almost as frustrating for teachers as it is for struggling students. Teachers cannot show their frustration. To reach every learner, they must be positive, patient, and creative in their teaching methods. Good communication skills also help students learn. In order to convey information and keep students interested, teachers should speak clearly and expressively.

A sense of humor is not a bad quality to have, either. Successful teachers often use humor to redirect inappropriate student behavior, relieve stress in the classroom, keep students interested, and create a comfortable atmosphere, all of which enhance learning.

Working Conditions

Most K–12 teachers work in schools. Some schools are bright and cheerful, while others are overcrowded and in poor condition. Generally, teachers have their own classroom. But it is not unusual for teachers in overcrowded buildings to share classrooms or move from room to room carrying their supplies on a rolling cart.

Traditionally, most teachers work ten months per year for a total of about 185 days, with a paid two-month break in the summer. Specific school calendars and school hours depend on the local school district. Usually, the day begins at 8:00 a.m. and ends at 3:00 p.m. However, many teachers arrive early and stay after hours to tutor students, meet with parents, sponsor clubs, or coach teams.

Employers and Pay

Most K–12 teachers are employed by public and private schools throughout the world. In fact, if you like to travel, the US Department of Defense and many private international schools employ American teachers abroad. Salaries vary. They are set by the school district or private school and depend on the location, the

Many Challenges

"The biggest challenge for me as an elementary school teacher is the diversity amongst the students. Diversity of languages is a very big one at our school as we have a lot of ELL [English language learner] students where English is their second language. There are also different levels in each classroom. . . . You have some kids who excel in certain areas, maybe math, where other kids are lower in math. It's the same thing with reading. . . . So you need to try and meet the needs of all those students."

Chris Flores, California third-grade teacher

Quoted in Teach California, "Teacher Interview with Chris Flores," 2018. www.teach california.org.

teacher's level of education, and length of service. According to the Bureau of Labor Statistics (BLS), salaries range from about $37,340 to about $95,380, with a median salary of $58,780. For the most part, all K–12 teachers in a school district follow the same salary scale. In addition to their wages, most teachers receive employee benefits that include health insurance, retirement benefits, and paid sick and vacation days. In addition, those who teach in low-income communities or in fields in which there is a shortage of qualified teachers—such as special education, bilingual education, English as a second language, foreign languages, math, and science—may qualify for full or partial student loan forgiveness.

What Is the Future Outlook for K–12 Teachers?

The BLS predicts that employment for K–12 teachers will grow by 7 percent to 8 percent through 2026, which is about as fast as average for all occupations. Job prospects should be greatest in teaching fields and geographic areas in which there are shortages. The latter include inner cities, rural areas, low-income schools, and in the South and the West. In addition, many individuals exit the field each year, leaving open positions. Therefore, if you want to positively contribute to the lives of children and adolescents, you should be warmly welcomed into the field.

Find Out More
American Federation of Teachers (AFT)
555 New Jersey Ave. NW
Washington, DC 20001
website: www.aft.org

The AFT is a labor union that represents teachers. It offers information about the profession and becoming a teacher.

Educators Rising
1820 N. Fort Myer Dr., Suite 320
Arlington, VA 22209
website: www.educatorsrising.org

Educators Rising is an organization that provides support and information for young people who are considering a teaching career. It offers an online library and videos, an annual conference, leadership opportunities, and thirty scholarships.

Future Educators
PO Box 7888
Bloomington, IN 47407
website: www.futureeducators.org

Future Educators is an organization that offers a wealth of information to help aspiring teachers explore the profession, including articles about what teachers do, how to succeed in the classroom, education and training, college life, and scholarships.

National Education Association (NEA)
1201 Sixteenth St. NW
Washington, DC 20036
website: www.nea.org

The NEA is an organization made up of professional educators. It sponsors a student program for aspiring teachers; publishes a brochure describing different aspects of the profession; and provides a wealth of information on topics such as getting a job, salaries, and student loans.

Registered Nurse

A Few Facts

Number of Jobs
About 2,955,200 as of 2016

Pay
About $48,690 to $104,100

Educational Requirements
Bachelor of science in nursing, associate's degree in nursing, or a nursing diploma from a hospital or medical center

Personal Qualities
Compassionate, detail oriented

Work Settings
Indoors in health care facilities, in patients' homes

Future Job Outlook
Projected 15 percent job growth through 2026

What Does a Registered Nurse Do?

If you've ever been ill or had a physical exam, odds are a registered nurse, or RN, helped take care of you. RNs are special people; they care for, advise, and support sick and injured individuals. It is not unusual for patients to consider a caring nurse their own guardian angel. Eileen Williamson, an RN, explains:

> We spend more time with patients than any other group in healthcare. We minister to, talk with, counsel, console and advise them. . . . It is the nurse who is charged with teaching patients about their illnesses and ensuring they understand their care plans. It is the nurse who provides them with information, explains procedures, presents options and alternatives, and answers their questions. It is the nurse who upholds patients' rights and serves as a liaison with their physicians and families.[33]

Working as part of a health care team, RNs observe, assess, and monitor the condition of each person in their care. They help administer and evaluate diagnostic tests, dispense medication, and educate patients and their loved ones about the patient's condition and how to cope with it, among other tasks.

RNs can be generalists or can choose to specialize in one or more of over ninety nursing specialties. Some specialty fields are determined by an RN's workplace, such as an emergency room nurse. Other specialties are determined by the health condition or type of patient, such as an oncology (dealing with cancer) nurse or a pediatric (dealing with children) nurse. But no matter the specialty area, if you decide to become a nurse, your work will make a difference in people's lives.

A Typical Workday

"Be prepared for the unexpected—Anything can happen at any moment,"[34] says Buffalo, New York, RN Alexander Alvaro Salinas. RNs care for lots of patients with diverse health issues, and emergencies can arise at any time. Every day is full of new and different challenges. However, there are certain tasks that most RNs perform on a daily basis. These include taking patients' vital signs, changing dressings, administering medication, and talking with patients and their families. Depending on their specialty field, they may also prepare patients for and assist during surgery, help deliver babies, or treat sick schoolchildren, just to name a few possibilities. No matter what else they do, one thing is a constant—RNs are always dealing with people. As Lisa McDew, a Minnesota RN, explains, "I interact with patients and their families, other nurses, nursing assistants, unit secretary, doctors, nurse practitioners, physician assistants, laboratory, radiology, spiritual care and healing healthcare staff, and social workers."[35]

Education and Training

If you decide to become a nurse, you can enter this field in several ways. One way is by attending an RN diploma program offered by

A Demanding Job

"Some days you walk in and you may not leave just one patient's room for three or four hours depending on how sick he or she is. I can't count the number of lunch breaks I've missed or the grab-and-go lunches I've stuffed in my mouth—I highly recommend learning how to eat a lunch in two minutes."

Allyson Lenoci, RN

Allyson Lenoci, "14 Things I Wish I Knew Before I Became a Nurse," *Cosmopolitan*, June 12, 2015. www.cosmopolitan.com.

hospitals. This usually takes one to three years of postsecondary training, depending on the program. Or you can earn an associate's degree in nursing from a community college, which usually takes two years of postsecondary education. Another way is by earning a bachelor of science degree in nursing from a college or university, which usually takes four years of postsecondary training. Many employers prefer that RNs have a bachelor's degree. Some offer RNs in their employ who have diplomas or associate's degrees tuition reimbursement benefits so that they can earn a bachelor's degree.

No matter which path you choose to follow, you can expect stiff competition for acceptance into the program. To prepare for these programs, in high school you should take courses in biology, health, and chemistry. And to make sure that nursing is the right choice for you, it is a good idea to volunteer in a hospital or other medical facility. Doing so not only gives you a chance to explore the profession, it looks great on a nursing school application.

Nursing school is rigorous. Course work includes classes in nursing theory and techniques, biology, chemistry, psychology, and physiology. Students also do supervised clinical practice in a variety of specialty fields. As Roya Shareefy, a graduate of Emory University's nursing school, recalls, "Being in nursing school was definitely my most challenging years. . . . I had to focus more on my studies than other aspects of life, and learn so much in a short amount of time. The clinical experience of nursing school allowed me to have the opportunity to put what I learned in my classes and readings into action."[36]

Upon graduating from an accredited nursing program, candidates must successfully complete a written exam administered by the National Council of State Boards of Nursing in order to be licensed. Most candidates pass the exam the first time they take it. Those who do not can retake the test.

Skills and Personality

If you like being on the go, nursing may be the career for you. RNs are almost always moving. Many work twelve-hour shifts with few breaks, and they stand, walk, bend, twist, stretch, and lift patients and equipment. To do their job effectively, nurses need physical stamina. As Washington, DC, RN Allyson Lenoci explains, "It's way more work than it looks like on paper. . . . There's virtually no downtime and you're physically on your feet, running around during the entire shift. I wear a FitBit and I can easily put on 5 miles in a single day."[37]

Compassion and emotional strength are also essential. When it comes to patient care, RNs are on the front lines. They frequently deal with patients who take their pain and frustration out on their caregivers. RNs must be emotionally strong; they cannot take such outbursts personally. In order to give every patient good care, even when patients are disrespectful, nurses have to be sympathetic and pleasant. As Kathleen Carlson, an emergency room RN, explains, "There's a lot of what we call 'violent verbal abuse' in our department. Patients might call you names, or take out their frustrations by yelling at you. I think everybody just has to put on their armor before coming to work."[38]

Emotional strength also comes into play when RNs encounter death. RNs care about their patients. Even when death is inevitable, losing a patient is difficult. Although RNs mourn these losses, they must be able to accept death without letting it impact their personal well-being or their ability to do their job. As Kathy Quan, who has been an RN for more than thirty years, explains, "The death of a patient is a harsh reality in nursing. Learning to deal with it and knowing what to expect is a necessary part of the job."[39]

Being detail oriented is another vital trait. When it comes to administering medicine or other treatments, nurses must be meticulous. Even small mistakes can put lives at risk. RNs should also be observant and have good listening skills. They use their eyes and their ears to obtain information from patients. Plus, by being good listeners, they let patients know that their concerns are being heard, which comforts patients and builds trust. Good speaking skills are also important. RNs explain medical procedures, treatments, and other issues to patients and their families. They must be able to do this in clear, understandable terms.

Working Conditions

If you decide to become an RN, you will probably work in a hospital or other health care facility, although some RNs travel to patients' homes. Approximately 80 percent of RNs work full time. Those who work in physicians' offices usually work a five-day, forty-hour workweek. Those who work in hospitals and other facilities that are open round-the-clock usually work twelve-hour rotating shifts for three or four days per week, including weekends, nights, and holidays. They may also be on call, which means they must be available to report to work whenever they are needed. As Carlson explains, "We . . . have on-call times, so you have to sign up for so many hours of on-call every six weeks—beyond your regular shifts—and be prepared to go into work at a moment's notice."[40]

Other working conditions can take a toll on a nurse's health. Long shifts, being on one's feet for extended periods, lifting and transferring patients, and exposure to infectious diseases are part of being an RN. It is not unusual for RNs to have foot, knee, and back problems. Wearing comfortable shoes, compression socks, gloves, and masks and practicing good body mechanics helps them reduce health risks.

Employers and Pay

Fifty percent of RNs are employed by hospitals. RNs are also employed by physicians' private practices, outpatient clinics, nursing homes, educational and correctional institutions, private businesses, the military, and public and home health agencies. If you enter this field, you should earn a comfortable income. According to the Bureau of Labor Statistics (BLS), as of 2017 the average median income for RNs was $70,000, with the lowest-paid 10 percent earning less than $48,690 and the highest-paid 10 percent earning more than $104,100. RNs usually get generous employee benefits, including health insurance, paid vacation and sick days, retirement benefits, and monetary sign-on bonuses when they are hired.

What Is the Future Outlook for RNs?

The future looks bright for RNs. The BLS predicts that employment for RNs will increase by 15 percent through 2026, which is faster than average. Plus, more than five hundred thousand RNs are expected to retire by 2022, which will create even more vacancies. Indeed, if you decide to become an RN, the odds of finding a job that suits you are in your favor.

Find Out More

All Nurses

website: https://allnurses.com

This is a social networking site in which nurses and nursing students learn from each other. It offers career advice, study and other tips for nursing and pre-nursing students, information about nursing school programs, scholarships, specialty fields, licensing exams, and job listings.

American Nurses Association (ANA)

8515 Georgia Ave., Suite 400
Silver Spring, MD 20910
website: www.nursingworld.org

The ANA is a large nursing association that offers information on a wide range of topics related to a career in nursing, including working conditions, licensing, scholarships, specialty fields, and nursing publications.

Discover Nursing

website: www.discovernursing.com

This website sponsored by Johnson & Johnson seeks to promote nursing as a career. It offers lots of information about nursing schools, scholarships, and nursing careers, as well as publications and interviews with nurses.

Nursing Link

website: http://nursinglink.monster.com

Nursing Link is a website for aspiring and current nurses. It gives information and advice about becoming an RN, nursing programs, characteristics of effective nurses, licensing exams, various specialties, job listings, and more.

Sales Representative

What Does a Sales Representative Do?

Sales representatives, also known as sales reps or sales consultants, sell almost any product or service you can imagine directly from manufacturers, producers, or wholesalers to retail stores, businesses, government agencies, and other organizations, rather than to individual consumers. For example, they sell musical instruments to music stores, drugs and medical equipment to hospitals, and machinery to factories. Most sales reps specialize in selling within a particular industry, which makes it possible for individuals with a particular interest to tailor their career in that direction. So if you love science, you can specialize in selling medical and pharmaceutical products to health care facilities. Or if fashion is your passion, you can specialize in selling designer creations to clothing stores, and so on.

Although selling is the essence of this occupation, there is a lot more to this job than meets the eye. Before sales reps can make a sale, they must identify and contact prospective customers. They do this in one of two ways. The first, known as cold calling, involves making unsolicited contact with strangers by phone, e-mail, social

52

media, and in person in an effort to persuade prospective clients to purchase whatever product or service the sales rep is selling. Sales reps also identify prospective customers through referrals or leads. If prospective clients show an interest in the product or service, sales reps set up a meeting in which they give a preplanned pre-sentation describing the sales product and how it can benefit the client, and they answer any questions the client may have.

Once a sale is made, sales reps keep in regular touch with clients, help them deal with any problems related to the product, and sometimes train them and their staff on how best to use the product. Providing stellar customer service helps sales reps build and maintain lasting relationships with their clients, which typi-cally translates into repeat sales. As Joe Camberato, president of National Business Capital, a company that sells financial services to businesses, explains, "Succeeding at sales requires taking the time to form relationships."[41]

A Typical Workday

Sales reps can be inside or outside sales reps. If you decide to become a sales rep, how you'll spend a typical workday will de-pend on which type of sales rep you are. Inside sales reps rarely meet with clients face-to-face. They spend most of their workday contacting prospective and existing clients by phone, e-mail, and social media and usually conduct meetings virtually.

Outside sales reps add a personal touch. They travel around an assigned territory, visiting prospective and existing clients. "I'm typically up around six o'clock, 6:30 and then heading out to some accounts and calling on the doctors," explains a medical device sales representative. "I typically get to about three or four [prospec-tive] accounts a day. . . . I also go to my accounts that I've already sold to and make sure that they're happy with the product."[42]

Despite differences in their workdays, all sales representatives share many tasks in common. Whether electronically or physi-cally, in a typical day, they make lots of cold calls, follow up on leads, and check in with existing clients. Plus, they do paperwork, including but not limited to keeping records of all their sales calls, filling out sales contracts, and scheduling deliveries.

Education and Training

There are a variety of ways you can enter this field. Educational requirements vary according to the particular industry or specialty field you represent. A minimum of a high school diploma is required for positions selling nontechnical or nonscientific products. Sales reps in technical and scientific sales need a bachelor's degree. These include sales reps of pharmaceutical goods, medical instruments, and technical and industrial equipment.

No matter what area of sales interests you, you can start preparing for this career in high school by taking classes in business, psychology, and economics. These help sales reps in dealing with clients and handling business transactions. Speech and drama classes are also useful. They enhance communication skills and build self-confidence, both of which are needed to communicate effectively with clients and give successful presentations.

Candidates interested in technical and scientific sales usually get a bachelor's degree in an area related to the industry or field they want to represent. For instance, those interested in pharmaceutical sales might major in chemistry or biology. Aspiring technical and scientific sales reps also take classes in psychology, business, and marketing.

Whether or not you attend college, having previous sales experience is important, too. It can be in a retail store or as part of a fund-raiser. This gives individuals a chance to see whether they like selling and provides them with valuable experience that can help them land a full-time position.

Skills and Personality

Sales reps interact with others constantly. If you decide this is the career for you, you should be personable and enjoy meeting new people. "You've gotta love people to do this job,"[43] says Pennsylvania sales rep Chuck Piola. Interpersonal skills are also essential in establishing and maintaining relationships with clients. Persuasiveness and self-confidence are vital, too. It takes lots of self-confidence to make cold calls and strong powers of persuasion to turn a stranger into a customer. It also takes persistence. Successful sales reps do not give up easily or take rejection personally. They keep cold-calling and following leads. According to Evan Marmott, the chief executive officer of two companies that sell financial services to businesses, "Persistency is really, really the key. . . . It's not always easy, but you've got to stay late, make the phone calls, send the emails and do the follow-ups. It's a numbers game."[44]

Being ambitious and motivated are other essential traits. Outside sales reps make their own schedules and are not closely supervised. This gives them a high level of control over their career, which is great for self-motivated, ambitious people but not so great if you are an individual that needs more supervision and structure to succeed. Moreover, all sales reps are expected to meet predetermined sales targets within a specified period of time. The more motivated the individual, the more likely he or she will meet or even beat sales goals.

Working Conditions

The work setting generally depends on whether you are doing inside or outside sales. Inside sales reps spend their workday in an office setting. They usually work a standard five-day, forty-hour workweek. Outside sales people spend a lot of time traveling to and visiting with prospective and current customers. If their assigned territory covers a large area, they may be away from home for extended periods of time, which can be disruptive to an individual's personal life. Many sales reps work more than forty hours per week, and it is not unusual for them to entertain clients on weekends or evenings.

If you decide to enter this field, you can expect to be under a great deal of pressure to perform. Meeting sales targets is stressful, especially since a sales rep's job security and earnings often depend on it. Marmott puts it this way: "You get to eat what you kill. If you're not killing anything, you don't get to eat."[45]

Employers and Pay

Almost every industry employs sales representatives. Some reps are employed by businesses to sell the merchandise the company produces. Other sales reps work for sales agencies that sell products and services for different manufacturers. Some individuals are self-employed. These independent sales reps contract with different companies to sell their services or products.

As a sales rep, you can earn a great deal of money or not much at all—depending on your employer and how much you sell. Sales reps who sell technical and scientific products generally make more money than those who sell other types of products. According to the Bureau of Labor Statistics (BLS), as of May 2017 sales reps earned anywhere from about $27,700 to $157,500, depending on the type of product being sold. Most, but not all, employers pay sales reps a base salary plus commissions, which is a set percentage of the value of their sales. As a pharmaceutical sales rep explains, "The more you sell the more you make, so the harder you work, the more money you make."[46]

In addition to these earnings, many companies offer top sellers large bonuses. Outside sales reps receive additional perks. They are often provided with a company car, a smartphone, and reimbursement for business expenses. Most employers also provide sales reps with health insurance and paid sick and vacation days. Self-employed individuals do not receive these benefits, and they are usually paid on commission only.

What Is the Future Outlook for Sales Representatives?

The BLS predicts that employment opportunities for sales reps will grow by 5 percent through 2026, which is about as fast as average. Competition for jobs with companies or agencies offering the best wages, commissions, and benefits can be fierce. Therefore, the first test of your sales ability may be landing one of these positions. But if this is the right career for you, even if you start with a less lucrative position, it is likely that over time your hard work will be rewarded. As Jimmy Van, the founder of SalesCareer.net, explains, "With a sales career . . . you are directly the person responsible for making things happen. . . . You have a much higher level of control of your career when compared to many other career choices."[47]

Find Out More

DECA
1908 Association Dr.
Reston, VA 20191
website: www.deca.org

DECA is an organization that helps educate and prepare high school and college students for sales, marketing, and other business careers. It offers members workshops, conferences, competitions, networking opportunities, leadership training, and scholarships.

Manufacturers' Agents National Association (MANA)
6321 W. Dempster St., Suite 110
Morton Grove, IL 60053
website: www.manaonline.org

MANA is an organization that helps connect independent (self-employed) manufacturers' sales representatives and employers. It offers many articles that provide information about a career as an independent manufacturer's representative, as well as a blog, podcasts, and tips on being self-employed.

National Association of Sales Professionals (NASP)
555 Friendly St.
Bloomfield Hills, MI 48341
website: www.nasp.com

NASP is an association made up of sales professionals. It offers articles about sales careers, online educational programs, webinars, podcasts, job postings, and résumé writing tips.

SalesCareer.net
website: http://salescareer.net

This website aims to help current and future sales professionals find and succeed in sales jobs. It provides sales career advice, job listings, interviews, résumé writing tips, and an informative blog.

Social Worker

A Few Facts

Number of Jobs
About 682,100 as of 2016

Pay
About $29,560 to $79,740

Educational Requirements
Bachelor's degree

Personal Qualities
Good listener, good problem-solving skills

Work Settings
Indoors in an office setting with travel to visit clients

Future Job Outlook
Projected 16 percent job growth through 2026

What Does a Social Worker Do?

Social workers, also known as caseworkers or case managers, are warriors for social justice. They help people in need cope with and overcome problems, become more self-sufficient, and improve their lives. Among other tasks, social workers connect people in danger of deportation with legal services, help unemployed individuals get job training, and find safe housing for the homeless and victims of domestic violence. They also are involved in adoption and foster care services; help formerly incarcerated people transition back into society; provide emotional support and individual, group, and family counseling to bereaved individuals and people with mental, emotional, and behavioral disorders or substance abuse problems; and connect people to resources that help them overcome their problems. For instance, social workers help teenage mothers stay in school by connecting them with day care services. They help the poor obtain social services, such as food stamps, welfare, and low-income housing. And they find homes for orphaned and abandoned children.

In any given day, social workers touch many lives for the better, and in the course of a career, they may help hundreds of people turn their lives around. As Lorrinda Janik, a 2016 graduate of North Carolina State University's School of Social Work, explains: "Society leads us to believe one person cannot make a difference. As social workers, we learn one person has the ability to change the world."[48] Indeed, if you are a person who wants to change the world for the better, social work may be the career path for you.

Most social workers specialize in a particular area of social work. So if you decide to become a social worker, you can choose your career path based on your interests, the type of people you want to help, or the type of environment you prefer to work in. For example, if you are interested in health care, as a medical social worker, you can serve sick, injured, and disabled individuals. Or if you like working with young people, you can become a school social worker or a child and family social worker. If psychology fascinates you, you can become a mental health or substance abuse social worker, or with a master's degree, you can become a clinical social worker. Clinical social workers are licensed to diagnose and treat people with mental, emotional, and behavior issues, much like a mental health counselor. And these are just a few of the possible options. As Ashley Osborne, a social work graduate of Arizona State University, says, "As a social worker, I can work in many different fields, with many different populations, performing many different job functions. . . . Social work is a career that you can make unique for yourself. You can strive to make changes that you are passionate about."[49]

A Typical Day

What social workers do in a typical day largely depends on their area of focus, but there are certain tasks that most social workers perform on any given day. These include meeting with clients to evaluate their needs and provide them with emotional support; connecting clients to services that can help them; checking in with clients to make sure their situation has improved; taking notes

Many Roles

"Among my varied tasks, I have driven clients to the hospital, gone camping with a youth group, organized a task force of mental health care providers, and provided crisis support for grieving teens. I know my experience is not unique, in that all social workers will face a wide range of challenges, big and small."

Sharon L. Young, clinical social worker

Sharon L. Young, "What Have You Learned?," *New Social Worker*, Summer 2014. www.socialworker.com.

and maintaining files on clients; and in the case of clinical social workers, providing psychotherapy services. They also attend meetings, visit clients in their place of residence, testify in court on behalf of clients, and meet with policy makers to advocate for programs and policies that improve social conditions. Here's how Elizabeth Kelley, a Washington, DC, medical social worker, describes her workday: "Each day starts with a team conference, with physicians, therapists, and case managers coming together to discuss patient progress and issues. During the rest of my day, I assess the needs of new patients, give updates to insurance companies, plan patient discharges, and act as a liaison between patients and families and their medical team."[50]

Education and Training

Social workers must be licensed. To become licensed, individuals must pass a state exam. In order to qualify for the exam, social workers must have a bachelor's degree. Clinical social workers need a master's degree.

If social work interests you, you can start getting ready for this career in high school by taking classes that prepare you for college, as well as classes that improve your communication skills. Social workers spend a lot of time speaking and listening to clients. To do their job effectively, they need good communication skills, which speech and language arts classes help develop. Biology

A social worker talks with a woman about the help she needs for herself and her family. Social workers interact with clients on a very personal level and sometimes about very emotional topics.

and psychology classes, too, are useful. They help social workers better understand the physical and emotional problems that their clients may have. In addition, if you hope to work with immigrants or in an area where many people do not speak English, studying a foreign language is helpful.

In college, most aspiring social workers pursue a bachelor of social work (BSW) or a degree in a related field like psychology or sociology. If you pursue a BSW, you'll take required liberal arts classes plus classes related to social work, such as courses in human behavior and social welfare law. You'll also do approximately four hundred to six hundred hours of fieldwork. This involves working in a community service organization under the supervision of an experienced professional.

Skills and Personality

Social work is a helping profession that involves lots of social interaction. If you are interested in becoming a social worker, you should be a tolerant person who has a strong desire to help people in need. Social workers serve people who have many problems and come from diverse backgrounds. Rather than passing judgment on their clients, social workers should be compassionate, nonjudgmental, and tolerant of all their clients, no matter the clients' life path or cultural values. As Neil Headman, assistant professor of human services at the University of Illinois–Springfield, says, "It doesn't matter who your client is. Everyone needs help."[51]

Having good communication skills is also vital. Social workers talk to and listen to clients about the problems the clients face. In order to understand their clients' needs, social workers must be good listeners. They should also have good oral and written communication skills so that they can clearly pass on information to their clients and assist clients with applications for social services. Having good communication and listening skills also helps social workers gain their clients' trust. Being patient, attentive, and compassionate also helps build trust.

In addition, social workers should be good problem solvers and critical thinkers. A significant part of their job is helping people work through problems. Social workers use logic and reasoning, combined with their problem-solving skills, to come up with different approaches and solutions to these problems.

Working Conditions

If you become a social worker, you'll probably work in an office setting. You will also spend time outside the office visiting clients. Most social workers work a five-day, forty-hour week. Some work evenings and weekends to accommodate their clients' schedules and are on call for emergencies. Self-employed social workers set their own hours.

This can be a very rewarding profession. However, it can also be stressful and emotionally draining, and there are safety concerns. Social workers work with people who are struggling with heartbreaking issues like homelessness, poverty, domestic violence, and child abuse. Working with people in crisis can take an emotional and mental toll on social workers. In addition, they make home visits to crime-ridden neighborhoods, which puts them at risk for job-related safety issues. As Carol Goertzel, president and chief executive officer of a social service agency in Holmes, Pennsylvania, says, "It's wonderful work, but it's not for everybody."[52]

Employers and Pay

Social workers are employed by social welfare agencies; local, state, and federal governments; hospitals and residential care facilities; prisons; and schools and as officers in the military. About 1 percent are self-employed.

This is not a profession that will make you rich, but most people do not go into social work for the money. According to the Bureau of Labor Statistics (BLS), as of May 2017 the median annual salary was $47,980, with the lowest-paid 10 percent earning less than $29,560 and the highest-paid 10 percent earning more than $79,740. Earnings depend on an individual's training and experience, the employer, and the location. Social workers usually get employee benefits, including health insurance and paid vacation and sick days. Self-employed social workers do not get benefits.

What Is the Future Outlook for Social Workers?

The BLS reports that the overall employment for social workers is projected to grow by 16 percent through 2026, which is faster than average for all occupations. Specific predictions vary by areas of specialization. For example, through 2026, employment opportunities for child and family social workers and school social workers are predicted to grow by 14 percent; for medical social workers by 20 percent; and for mental health social workers and substance abuse social workers by 19 percent. So if you decide that this diverse helping profession is right for you, it is likely that you will be welcomed into the field.

Find Out More

Council on Social Work Education (CSWE)
1701 Duke St., Suite 200
Alexandria, VA 22314
website: www.cswe.org

The CSWE is an organization that supports social work education. It provides a listing of accredited social work programs on its website. It has a large section just for students that gives information on what social workers do, how to prepare for this career, and advice from social workers.

National Association of Social Workers (NASW)
750 First St. NE, Suite 800
Washington, DC 20002
website: www.socialworkers.org

The NASW is the largest professional organization of social workers in the world. It has state chapters and offers information about diverse social work careers, licensing, resources for students, job links, and social work news, and it sponsors a national conference.

Social Work Career

website: www.socialwork.career

Social Work Career is a blog full of information about a career in social work. It includes interviews with social workers, tips on finding a job, information about social work programs and licensing tests, and lots of articles and webinars.

Social Work License Map

website: https://socialworklicensemap.com

This website provides information about how to become a social worker, social work specialties, scholarships, salaries, and state licensing.

Source Notes

A Big Decision

1. Catherine Lovering, "The Advantages of Following Your Interests in a Career," *Chron*, 2018. https://work.chron.com.
2. Quoted in Erik J. Martin, "In a Job Search, Social Skills Matter," AARP, December 6, 2016. www.aarp.org.
3. Mary Dowd, "The Importance of Choosing a Career Path," *Chron*, June 30, 2018. https://work.chron.com.

Event Planner

4. Quoted in Danielle McIntyre, "Student Feature—Lauren Spingola," *Pointers for Planners* (blog), QC Event School, February 12, 2018. https://blog.qceventplanning.com.
5. Quoted in Charyn Pfeuffer, "Seven Jobs for Social Butterflies," Monster, 2018. www.monster.com.
6. Danielle Nunez Seaberg, "What Does an Event Planner Really Do?," LinkedIn, December 6, 2014. www.linkedin.com.
7. Melanie Woodward, "5 Event Planning Skills You Need for Success," Balance Small Business, April 19, 2018. www.the balancesmb.com.
8. Quoted in Jennifer Alyson, "How Does an Event Planner Spend a Workday?," *Chron*, 2018. https://smallbusiness .chron.com.
9. Quoted in Tom Crowl, "Event Planning Tips with Melanie Woodward," *The Savvy Event Planner Podcast*, 2018. http:// savvyeventpodcast.com.

Fitness Trainer and Instructor

10. Quoted in Sandy Reimer, "Why I Love Being a Personal Trainer," YWCA Metro Vancouver, June 11, 2015. https://ywca van.org.
11. Quoted in Kathleen Greene, "My Career," *Occupational Outlook Quarterly*, Winter 2012–2013. www.bls.gov.

12. Quoted in Greene, "My Career."
13. Anita Lemon, "10 Personality Traits Top Personal Trainers Possess," Academy of Fitness Professionals, June 24, 2015. www.academyoffitnessprofessionals.com.
14. Lisa M. Wolfe, "What Are the Hours for a Personal Trainer?," Livestrong.com, January 30, 2018. www.livestrong.com.

Hairstylist and Barber

15. Barb Quinn, "Why I Love Being a Hair Stylist," EQ School of Hair Design, February 20, 2015. www.eqschool.net.
16. Quoted in Tricia Chaves, "What Are Five Tasks Performed Daily as a Hair Stylist?," *Chron*, 2018. https://work.chron.com.
17. Quoted in Kayleen Schaefer, "Your Hairdressers Know, but They're Not Talking," *New York Times*, December 6, 2007. www.nytimes.com.
18. Quoted in Momentum, "The Monday Interview—'So, What's It Really Like Working as a . . . Hairdresser?,'" April 29, 2018. www.momentumcareersadvice.com.
19. Quoted in Lucia Quinonez, "A Childhood Dream of Becoming a Hairstylist Led to a Lifelong Career in Cosmetology," *Borderzine*, February 1, 2013. http://borderzine.com.
20. Quoted in Bean, "A Day in the Life of a Hair Stylist," Edu Connect, July 28, 2016. https://educonnect.co.za.

Human Resources Specialist

21. Quoted in Melissa Suzuno, "Thinking of Working in HR? What You Need to Know," *After College* (blog), June 11, 2014. http://blog.aftercollege.com.
22. Quoted in Ben Eubanks, "A Day in the Life of a Human Resources Manager," *upstartHR* (blog), May 2015. https://upstarthr.com.
23. Sharlyn Lauby, "Ask HR Bartender: A Day in the Life of Human Resources," HR Bartender, June 19, 2011. www.hrbartender.com.
24. Quoted in Eubanks, "A Day in the Life of a Human Resources Manager."
25. Quoted in Eubanks, "A Day in the Life of a Human Resources Manager."

26. Quoted in Eubanks, "A Day in the Life of a Human Resources Manager."

K–12 Teacher

27. Quoted in Job Shadow, "Interview with a Band Director," 2012. https://jobshadow.com.
28. Quoted in Katrina Fried, "21 Reasons to Quit Your Job and Become a Teacher," *Huffington Post*, December 16, 2013. www.huffingtonpost.com.
29. Quoted in Job Shadow, "Interview with a 3rd Grade Teacher," 2012. https://jobshadow.com.
30. Quoted in Job Shadow, "Interview with a Biology Teacher," 2012. https://jobshadow.com.
31. Quoted in Teacher Certification Degrees, "Interview with Dana Lester, Tennessee First Grade Teacher," 2018. www.teacher certificationdegrees.com.
32. Quoted in Teacher Certification Degrees, "Interview with Alicia Lochridge, Nevada First Grade Teacher," 2018. www.teacher certificationdegrees.com.

Registered Nurse

33. Eileen Williamson, "If You're a Nurse, You're a Patient Advocate," Nurse.com, July 26, 2018. www.nurse.com.
34. Alexander Alvaro Salinas, "My First Year as a Nurse Was a Roller Coaster Ride," Nurse.com, May 21, 2018. www.nurse.com.
35. Quoted in Nancy Crotti, "All in a Day's Work: Registered Nurse," *Minneapolis (MN) Star Tribune*, March 25, 2009. www.startribune.com.
36. Roya Shareefy, "My Experiences as a Student Nurse," Emory Nursing, April 10, 2017. www.emorynursingnow.com.
37. Allyson Lenoci, "14 Things I Wish I Knew Before I Became a Nurse," *Cosmopolitan*, June 12, 2015. www.cosmopolitan.com.
38. Quoted in Arielle Pardes, "10 Things I Wish I Knew Before I Became an Emergency Room Nurse," *Cosmopolitan*, December 13, 2016. www.cosmopolitan.com.

39. Kathy Quan, "How to Deal with a Patient's Death," Nursing Link, 2018. http://nursinglink.monster.com.
40. Quoted in Pardes, "10 Things I Wish I Knew Before I Became an Emergency Room Nurse."

Sales Representative

41. Quoted in Ed McKinley, "Grooming the Best Sales Reps," Debanked, August 22, 2018. https://debanked.com.
42. Quoted in Job Shadow, "An Interview with a Medical Device Sales Consultant," 2012. https://jobshadow.com.
43. Quoted in Jay Finegan, "48 Hours with the King of Cold Calling," *Inc.*, June 1, 1991. www.inc.com.
44. Quoted in McKinley, "Grooming The Best Sales Reps."
45. Quoted in McKinley, "Grooming The Best Sales Reps."
46. Quoted in Job Shadow, "Interview with Pfizer Pharmaceutical Rep," 2012. https://jobshadow.com.
47. Jimmy Van, "Why a Career in Sales: Pros and Cons," Sales Career.net, 2017. http://salescareer.net.

Social Worker

48. Lorrinda Janik, "One Social Worker Can Make a Difference— Supporting Nontraditional Students," *New Social Worker*, 2016. www.socialworker.com.
49. Ashley Osborne, "Social Work—Making the World a Better Place," *New Social Worker*, 2016. www.socialworker.com.
50. Quoted in Sara Royster, "Interview with a Social Worker," Bureau of Labor Statistics, November 2015. www.bls.gov.
51. Quoted in *Occupational Outlook Quarterly*, "Helping Those in Need," Fall 2011. www.bls.gov.
52. Quoted in *Occupational Outlook Quarterly*, "Helping Those in Need."

Interview with a Hairstylist

Hector Maese is a self-employed hairstylist in Las Cruces, New Mexico. He has worked as a hairstylist for fifty years. He answered questions about his career in a personal interview with the author.

Q: Why did you become a hairstylist?

A: I went into the Navy right after high school. I was a radar technician. At the time, when we were in port we weren't allowed to get off the ship if our hair was too long and we had any hair around our ears. I had a brother-in-law that was a barber. When I went home on leave, he gave me a pair of shears and a couple of lessons about how to clean up around the ears. So, I started working on the guys in my division. Every time we pulled into port, I would clean the guys up around their ears with my shears. They'd leave a couple of bucks in my sailor's cap, and it was fun. When I got out of the Navy I tried to get a job as a civilian radar or electronic technician at White Sands [an army missile testing range located near his hometown], but there were no positions. I'd been in Vietnam, and now I wanted to be home. My brother-in-law had a barbershop. I thought I'd take some classes at the university and also get my barber's license. That way, I could stay in my home town, go to college, and work in my brother-in-law's shop on weekends to earn some money.

I never thought I'd ever be a full-time barber, but I saw an opportunity to feed myself by working part time while I went to college. So, I got my barber's license, which took me three months instead of six months because I went to beauty school double-time. I passed the licensing test with flying colors. The test is both a written and practical test. You actually have to cut hair for the examiners. So, I became a licensed barber and hairdresser.

Then I got my master's license eighteen months later. My brother-in-law became my mentor. I worked for him for three and a half years. Then, when he and my sister moved out of town, I opened my own shop. I decided to limit my shop to shampoo, cut, and blow dry only—hairstylist—no barbering, no coloring, no perms. I worked as hard as I could. I delayed taking more college classes; instead I attended a lot of different seminars on hairstyling and business and I learned.

Q: Can you describe your typical workday?

A: I work from eight a.m. to six p.m., Tuesday through Friday, and half day on Saturday. Ideally, you want to have one client an hour, but that's dreaming. Usually I see three to four clients per day, for an hour per client. But I'm not a typical hairstylist; I'm working at a high level. I'm a specialist with a one-person shop, and my prices reflect my expertise. Between clients I clean up the bathroom, floors, mirrors; I order and pick up supplies; and I take care of all the paperwork of running a business, and do general chores. I don't do the same thing every day; it depends on how busy I am. Every day is different.

Q: What do you like most about your job?

A: This is my attitude about my job: My job is like going to college and getting paid to learn, because I learn something from every one of my clients about business and life. And, that's what kept me in this job. Also, this job is like going to a health club and getting paid to work out. I'm sweeping, washing hair, standing, moving around, and that keeps me in shape and adds quality to my day. I have quality every day and I don't get bored. I also like that I am a one-man operation; I control my space and my schedule.

Q: What do you like least about your job?

A: I work by appointment only. I don't mind people calling up and cancelling. If something comes up, I understand. But I don't like it when people don't show up for an appointment and don't bother to call and cancel. It's wasted time.

Q: What personal qualities do you find most valuable for this type of work?

A: Good health—you have to be in good condition to do what I do. I prepare mentally and physically to be the best every day. I stay in shape. I stay well. Also, you need good communication skills. That's why I took a business communication class. It's one of the best investments I ever made.

Q: What advice do you have for students who might be interested in this career?

A: Never stop learning. I took business, communication, and psychology classes. I read lots of books on business. Also, hone your communication skills and dress for success. Don't get greedy. Pay attention to your clients. Use common sense, and be realistic. Put yourself in other people's shoes. Treat your clients the way you want them to treat you. And remember, 99 percent of success is showing up, and 100 percent is showing up on time.

Other Careers If You Like Social Interaction

Arbitrator

Chiropractor

Clergyperson

Computer support specialist

Customer service
  representative

Dental hygienist

Dentist

Emergency medical technician

Financial adviser

Flight attendant

Food and beverage server

Funeral director

Guidance counselor

Home health aide

Insurance agent

Lawyer

Life coach

Marketing manager

Occupational therapist

Office manager

Pharmacy technician

Physical therapist

Physician

Physician assistant

Police officer

Psychologist

Public relations specialist

Real estate agent

Receptionist

Retail salesperson

School administrator

Speech therapist

Tour guide

Editor's note: The online *Occupational Outlook Handbook* of the US Department of Labor's Bureau of Labor Statistics is an excellent source of information on jobs in hundreds of career fields, including many of those listed here. The *Occupational Outlook Handbook* may be accessed online at www.bls.gov/ooh.

Index

Note: Boldface page numbers indicate illustrations.

Picture Credits

About the Author

Barbara Sheen is the author of 102 books for young people. She lives in New Mexico with her family. In her spare time, she likes to swim, walk, garden, and cook.